DUST STORMS:
CAUSES AND EFFECTS

by Margaret Williamson

12 STORY LIBRARY
MORE TO EXPLORE

www.12StoryLibrary.com

12-Story Library is an imprint of Bookstaves.

Developed and produced for 12-Story Library by Focus Strategic Communications Inc.

Library of Congress Cataloging-in-Publication Data
Names: Williamson, Margaret (Elementary school teacher), author.
Title: Dust storms : causes and effects / by Margaret Williamson.
Description: Mankato, Minnesota : 12-Story Library, [2022] | Series: Wild weather |
Includes bibliographical references and index. | Audience: Ages 10–13 | Audience: Grades 4–6
Identifiers: LCCN 2020017446 (print) | LCCN 2020017447 (ebook) | ISBN 9781645821465 (library binding) | ISBN 9781645821847 (paperback) | ISBN 9781645822196 (pdf)
Subjects: LCSH: Dust storms—Juvenile literature.
Classification: LCC QC958 .W55 2022 (print) | LCC QC958 (ebook) | DDC 551.55/9—dc23
LC record available at https://lccn.loc.gov/2020017446
LC ebook record available at https://lccn.loc.gov/2020017447

Photographs ©: Caleb Holder/Shutterstock.com, cover, 1, 4; Oleg Golovnev/Shutterstock.com, 5; John D Sirlin/Shutterstock.com, 5; Minerva Studio/Shutterstock.com, 6; Stefano Garau/Shutterstock.com, 6; NOAA, 7; North Wind Picture Archives/Alamy, 8; iko/Shutterstock.com, 8; Everett Historical/Shutterstock.com, 9; National Archives and Records Administration, 9; vincent369/Shutterstock.com, 10; Jina K/Shutterstock.com, 10; NASA, 11; Maxim Petrichuk/Shutterstock.com, 11; Walkabout Photo Guides/Shutterstock.com, 12; JordiStock/Shutterstock.com, 13; totajla/Shutterstock.com, 13; NOAA, 14; NASA/Bill White, 15; NASA/NOAA/Naval Research Laboratory Monterey/JPL-Caltech, 15; Elizaveta Galitckaia/Shutterstock.com, 16; Pascal Mannaerts/Alamy, 17; Nephron/CC3.0, 17; Yerbolat Shadrakhov/Shutterstock.com, 18; John D Sirlin/Shutterstock.com, 19; Kevin Norris/Shutterstock.com, 19; SeaWiFS Project, NASA/Goddard Space Flight Center, 20; Steve Bower/Shutterstock.com, 21; D-VISIONS/Shutterstock.com, 21; Penny Compton 17/Shutterstock.com, 22; Chris Singshinsuk/Shutterstock.com, 23; mkldesigns/Shutterstock.com, 23; alexmak7/Shutterstock.com, 24; ArCaLu/Shutterstock.com, 25; Sophie Shoesmth/Shutterstock.com, 25; Vadim Sadovski/Shutterstock.com, 26; Purestock/Alamy, 27; Dotted Yeti/Shutterstock.com, 27; KevinRimcoski/Shutterstock.com, 28; Adisorn Kongprasert/Shutterstock.com, 29; aguarnaha/Shutterstock.com, 29

About the Cover

A dust storm approaches a town.

Access free, up-to-date content on this topic plus a full digital version of this book. Scan the QR code on page 31 or use your school's login at 12StoryLibrary.com.

Table of Contents

1

What Is This Wild Weather?

Fierce winds scrape dust from the dry ground. The gritty clouds swell into a dust storm. Dust storms are common in flat, dry areas with few trees. They occur all over the world, including in the US.

Dust storms can reach up to one mile (1.6 km) high. They travel between 25 to 60 miles

An approaching dust storm.

Dust storms can hurt people's eyes.

per hour (40 to 100 km/h). Some storms last for only a few minutes. Others can last for days.

Dust storms can be dangerous. They can make it hard to see when you are driving. The dust can get in your eyes and nose. If it gets into your lungs, you can have trouble breathing.

44 billion

Weight of dust in pounds (20 billion kg) found in the air

- Dead skin cells are found in dust.
- Some pieces of dust are so tiny they can't be seen.
- Small pieces of dust can stay in the air for 20 days.

HABOOB: IS THAT A REAL WORD?

Haboob is another name for a dust storm. It is pronounced *huh-boob*. It comes from the Arab word *habb*, which means wind or blow. Haboobs occur in Arizona and New Mexico. They also occur in the Middle East.

2

Wet or Dry: Downbursts and Dust Storms

Strong winds can turn thunderstorms into tornadoes. These winds spin. Thunderstorms can also create straight-line winds. Heavy rainfall drags the wind straight down. This downburst of air slams into the ground like a dropped glass of water. Gravity pulls the glass down. When it hits the floor, the water sprays out in all directions.

Downbursts can be wet or dry. A wet downburst brings wind and rain. Dry downbursts rip cloud bottoms into virga. Virga are thin sheets of moisture. Because the air in the

A downburst over a city.

downburst heats up, virga dry up and never touch the ground.

Dry downbursts cause dust storms. When the dry downburst hits the ground, it spreads out in all directions. It picks up dirt and creates a dust storm or *haboob*.

100

Speed in miles per hour (161 km/h) of a downburst

- A *microburst* is a small downburst.
- One downburst is blamed for a plane crash in 1985.
- As the plane landed, a microburst knocked it onto a highway.

The plane burst into flames and 137 people died.

3

Beware of Black Blizzards

Farmers tending to wheat, circa 1800.

In the late 1800s, US settlers moved onto the Great Plains. They came to farm the land. Before that, tall grasses covered the plains. Livestock grazed on the grassland.

FARMERS FLEE THE DUST BOWL

When the drought hit, many farmers fled the Great Plains. They headed to California to find work. They were not treated well. They were nicknamed Okies.

Heavy rains made the soil perfect for farming. By the 1920s, farmers used new inventions to grow bigger crops. Wheat replaced the grasses. The farmers earned lots of money, but the land suffered.

A drought hit the region in 1931. Droughts occur when no rain falls. After the wheat harvest, the hot sun baked the bare ground. Strong winds churned the topsoil. The skies filled with black blizzards. The Great Plains transformed into the Dust Bowl.

1935

Year of the worst Black Blizzard

- April 14, 1935, was named Black Sunday.
- A sunny afternoon turned black as night.
- Wind reached speeds up to 60 miles per hour (100 km/h).

4

Dust Storms Are a Global Hazard

A dust storm that hit China, 2010.

Earth's Northern Hemisphere has a dust belt. That is, many regions there are very dry and hot. They often undergo droughts. As a result, dust storms are common along Africa's west coast. They often strike the Middle East. They also happen in China.

Many dust storms start in the Sahara and Asian deserts.

Saharan dust storms affect Europe. They coat large areas with orange sand and dust. Yellow dust storms come from the dry regions in China. They blow pollution into Korea.

Asia and India are seeing more major dust storms. Deserts are expanding in these regions. In China, many areas are over-farmed. The land is overgrazed.

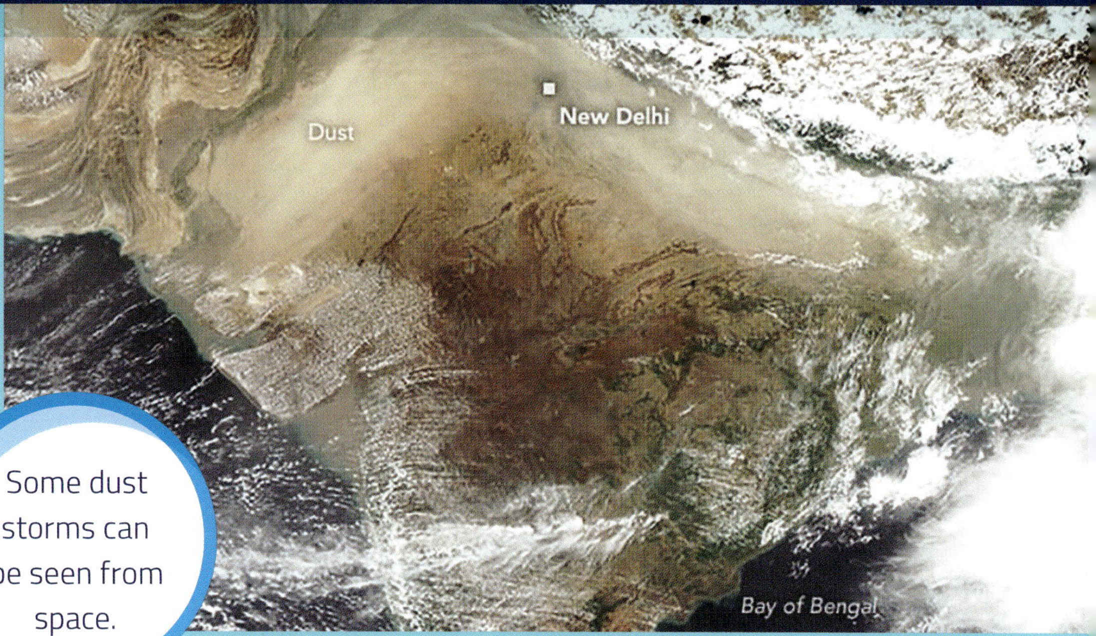

Some dust storms can be seen from space.

Rainfall is rare. High winds peel away soil and create massive dust storms.

Dust storms can be severe. In 2018, powerful dust storms hit India. More than 125 people died. Two hundred more were injured.

THINK ABOUT IT

What major dust events have occurred in the past five years? Where did they take place?

12

Number of hours a series of dust storms raged across Western Asia

- The dust event occurred in May 2018.
- Winds moved as fast as cars at 70 miles per hour (110 km/h).
- The storms knocked down 8,000 power poles.

5

Dust Devils Are Tiny Twisters

A dust devil.

A dust devil is a mini dust storm. It is a whirlwind that sucks dirt and dust from the ground. It moves the hazy grit to another area just like a dust storm does.

Dust devils are common on a clear, sunny day.

A dust devil forms when a small area heats up suddenly. For example, imagine dirt on a baseball diamond heating

up in the sun. The grassy outfield stays cool. The heat rises off the ground. It spins into a column. Like a drill, the hot air pokes a hole in the cooler air. The swirling air gathers dust from the baseball diamond. If air currents move the column, then the dust devil dances.

1,000

Height in feet (300 m) a dust devil can reach

- Dust devils occur in Texas in the warm summer months.
- They are common in dry regions of the world.
- Australians call these whirlwinds *willy-willy*.

6

Warning, Warning: Satellite Predictions

A GOES-R satellite.

The first GOES satellite was sent into space in 1975. The acronym stands for Geostationary Operational Environmental Satellite. This satellite helped scientists predict all types of wild weather. But it was slow to send pictures to Earth. It was hard for scientists to see dust storms. The dust was the same color as the ground.

This newest GOES-R satellite was sent into space in 2018. NASA built and launched

IT GOES ON AND ON

GOES satellites are used to track distress signals. They can help find airplanes or ships in trouble. GOES-T will launch in 2021. GOES-U heads to space in 2024.

this satellite. It has a special camera called an ABI. This camera snaps clear pictures of the Earth. Scientists can see landmarks. They can follow all kinds of weather. They are now able to predict a dust storm. They can also see volcanic ash and wildfires.

Hurricane Florence as seen from a GOES-R satellite.

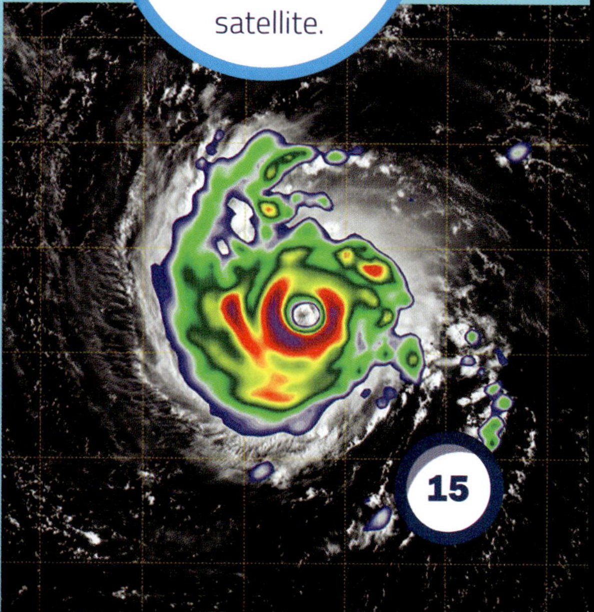

4

Number of the GOES satellites currently circling Earth

- One satellite sends pictures to Earth every 30 seconds.
- The satellite data creates public storm warnings that save many lives.
- It also helps firefighters fight forest fires.

7 The Threat From Dust Inside and Out

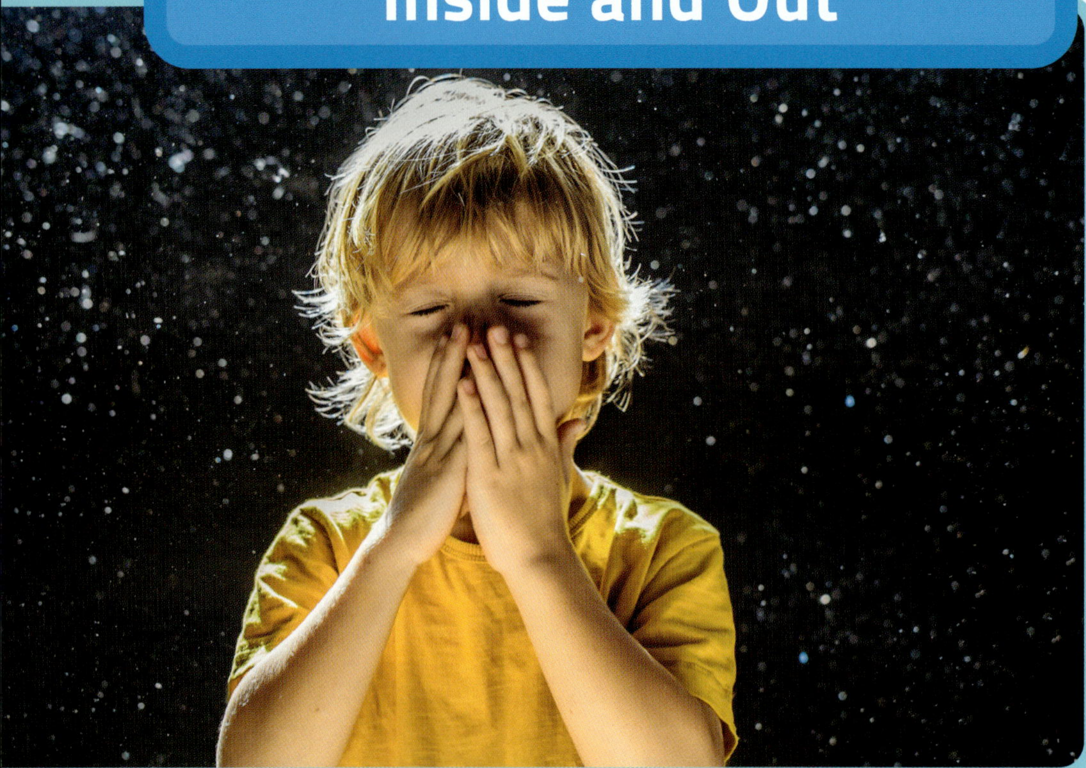

Dust is everywhere. No matter how often you try to sweep it away, it returns. But did you know that some dust can be dangerous to people's health?

After a dust storm is over, particles stay in the air. This dust can make people cough and sneeze. It can cause breathing problems. Dust has all sorts of harmful matter in it. The matter is what makes some people sick.

Valley fever is an illness that can be caused by dust storms. It is like a flu. It is caused by breathing in a mold that lives in the soil. The mold settles

A dust storm in Murghab, Tajikistan, 2016.

in the lungs. The sickness causes fever, body pain, and coughing. It can cause chills and headaches. A few people get a painful red rash. Valley fever attacks people who live in dust storm areas.

THINK ABOUT IT

How can you keep yourself safe from illnesses that dust can cause?

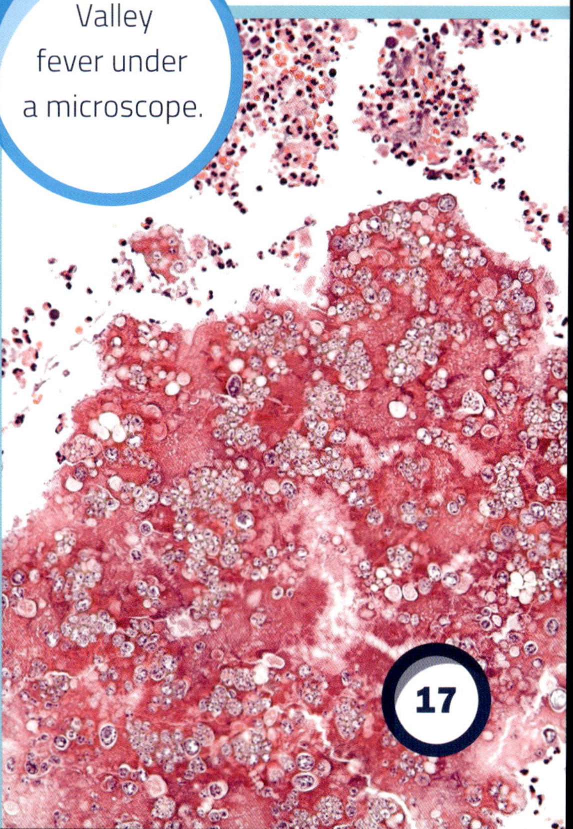

Valley fever under a microscope.

14,364

Number of valley fever cases reported in the US in 2017

- People who are over 60 tend to get valley fever.
- Pets can get valley fever.
- You can't catch valley fever from other people.

8

Dust and Sand: What's the Difference?

A sandstorm is a different kind of dust storm. Dust particles are like powder. Sand particles are bigger. They are like tiny beads. Sand forms as rocks chip apart or erode. The process can take millions of years.

Most often, sand gathers on beaches. It also covers desert regions.

A sandstorm moving into Arizona.

In a sandstorm, dry winds blast the sand off the ground. Sand can blow as high as 10 to 50 feet (3 to 15 m).

Most sandstorms travel at about 25 miles per hour (40 km/h). That is as fast as a Great White Shark.

3

Ranking of a sandstorm as the most dangerous weather in Arizona

- Blinding sand causes fatal car accidents.
- Sandstorms can make people sick.
- Sand can clog plane engines.

9

SAL Is Nature's Helpful Dust Storm

A dust storm over the Sahara Desert.

A large dust storm blows across the Atlantic Ocean every 3 to 5 days. The storm comes from the Sahara Desert. Weather watchers call the dust storm SAL. That stands for Saharan Air Layer. Strong winds push SAL high into the atmosphere.

4,000

Distance in miles (6,500 km) SAL sails across the Atlantic Ocean

- Dust from SAL makes rainforest soil more fertile.
- SAL brings beautiful sunsets to the Gulf Coast.
- In 2019, SAL turned the sky yellow in east Texas.

Scientists believe SAL has an interesting effect on wild weather. The dry air and dust that it carries prevent storms from forming over the Atlantic. Hurricanes don't like dry air. SAL's windy muscles can change air currents and slow hurricane winds.

Calima looks like dusty fog.

WHEN THE SAHARA WIND BLOWS

Calima is a wind current that brings hot weather and dust to the Canary Islands from the Sahara. It is a Spanish word that means *haze*. Calima is a dry fog. That is, it removes moisture from the air. Dust covers the islands. It can cause breathing difficulties. Fires spark more easily in these dry conditions.

10

Dust Storms Are A Complicated Part of the Environment

Dust storms are bad for the environment. Dust storms affect travel. They can make driving or walking difficult. They can cause flight delays. Dust jams mechanical parts in aircrafts. It can damage car engines. If dust storms blow topsoil from fields, then the bare land cannot support healthy plants or crops.

Dust is not healthy. Dust storms carry pollution over long distances. Dust makes people cough. It makes breathing hard for people with asthma. Humans and animals can get skin rashes. Dust irritates the eyes, too.

Dust storms can cause many health issues.

But did you know that dust storms have some positive effects, as well? Oceans benefit from dust storms. The dust helps plankton to grow. It contains nutrients that feed marine plants. Saharan dust fertilizes the Amazon rainforests. In 2017, a study found dust from the Gobi Desert in California. This dust helps fertilize the giant sequoia trees.

Sequoia trees.

2009

Year of the Red Dawn dust storm in Australia

- People woke up to a red sky filled with dust.
- Winds hauled 2.8 million tons (2.5 million metric tons) of soil off Australia's coastlines.
- Luckily, that dust fed plankton in the Tasman Sea. Plankton stores carbon and reduces climate change.

11

Desertification Has a Cause and Effect

Swampland.

Drylands are areas that get little rain. They are hot. Plants and animals have learned to survive there. But when people move there, they change the balance. They don't try to fit in to the environment. They change it to fit their needs.

Desertification results from ruined drylands. It is a serious environmental problem. Overpopulation harms dryland areas. Farming kills native plants. Water sources disappear. Finally, the soil supports no life. Harsh winds scrub the regions bare.

Desertification fuels more dust storms. Lots of soil is lost from the drylands. This blowing

dust affects people's health in nearby cities. It tangles traffic. It can cause power outages.

THINK ABOUT IT

What steps can be taken to change desertification?

Powerlines can get damaged during dust storms.

41

Percent of land on Earth that is dryland

- Each dryland has its own ecosystem.
- Almost half of Earth's dryland cannot support any towns or cities.
- People who live in drylands are often poor.

12

Out of This World: Dust Storms in Space

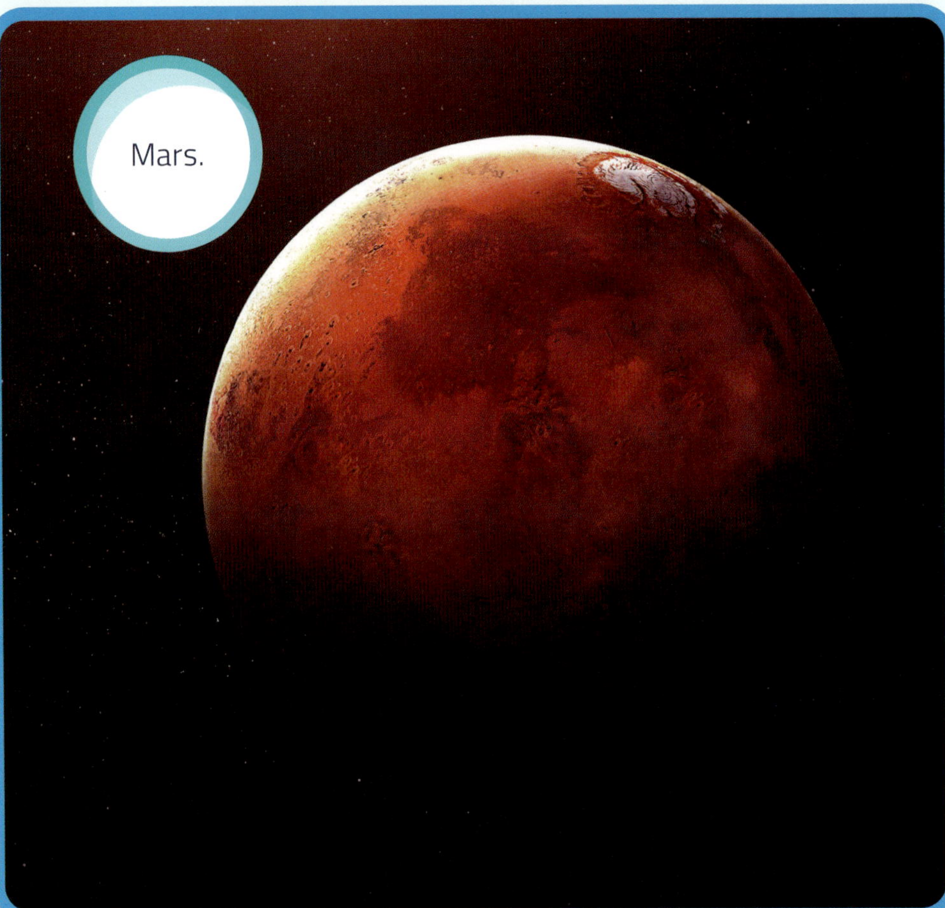

Mars.

Mars is a cold, dry planet. Dust storms are common. Most of these storms are small. Sometimes they join together. When they join, they surround the planet in a cloud of dust. This is called a global dust storm.

The Mars Rover.

835

Number of recovery commands sent to a Mars Rover in 2018

- The rover was named *Opportunity.*
- It worked on Mars for 15 years.
- It sent many pictures of Martian dust devils back to Earth.

In 2018, a global dust storm charged across Mars. Scientists lost contact with one of their rovers. The dust was very thick. The solar panel on the rover couldn't recharge.

Dust devils are also common on Mars. They form exactly like dust devils on Earth. They happen during Mars' summer months. These dust devils leave patterns in the soil of the planet. These devils are much taller than dust devils on Earth. The largest ones can reach heights of 5 miles (8 km).

WHY IS MARS RED?

Scientists have always been interested in Mars. It is called the Red Planet because red dust covers the entire planet. The soil on the surface has a red tinge because of rusting iron in the rocks.

Staying Safe in a Dust Storm

If you are driving and a dust storm hits, here is a list of things to do:

- Pull off the road to a safe spot or exit the highway.
- Put the car in park.
- Buckle up.
- Turn off all the lights.
- Be patient. Stay where you are until the storm passes.

Sometimes it's impossible to stop. If that happens,

- Drive slowly.
- Make sure your lights are flashing.
- Honk the horn often.

Hazard lights are important when a car needs to stop for an emergency.

The most important thing to remember is to never stop on the highway.

If you have to go out in a dust storm, cover your face with a scarf. Wear goggles to protect your eyes.

Glossary

asthma
A condition that makes it difficult for someone to breathe.

drought
A long period of time with very little or no rain.

ecosystem
Everything that exists in a particular environment.

fertilizer
Material that contains food for plants.

gravity
The force that causes things to fall toward the Earth.

hemisphere
A half of the Earth.

nutrient
Material, such as minerals or vitamins, that is found in foods.

plankton
The very small animal and plant life in bodies of water.

rover
An exploration vehicle that travels on the surface of Mars.

satellite
A machine that is sent into space and that moves around the Earth, Moon, Sun, or a planet.

virga
Drops of precipitation that evaporate before reaching the ground.

whirlwind
A very strong wind that moves in a spinning or swirling motion.

Read More

Arlon, Penelope, and Tory Gordon-Harris. *Weather*. New York City, NY: Scholastic, 2013.

Butterfield, Moira. *Weather: The Powerful Forces and Fragile Resources of Earth*. London, UK: Ticktock, 2015.

Farndon, John. *Weather*. New York City, NY: DK Publishing, 2017.

Rattini, Kristin Baird. *Weather*. National Geographic. Washington DC: 2013.

Visit 12StoryLibrary.com

Scan the code or use your school's login at **12StoryLibrary.com** for recent updates about this topic and a full digital version of this book. Enjoy free access to:

- **Digital ebook**
- **Breaking news updates**
- **Live content feeds**
- **Videos, interactive maps, and graphics**
- **Additional web resources**

Note to educators: Visit 12StoryLibrary.com/register to sign up for free premium website access. Enjoy live content plus a full digital version of every 12-Story Library book you own for every student at your school.

Index

About the Author

Margaret Williamson is a retired elementary school teacher. She enjoys music, crafting, writing for children, and watching sappy movies.